FISHING

OUTDOOR ADVENTURES

DAVID ARMENTROUT

The Rourke Press, Inc.
Vero Beach, Florida 32964

© 1998 The Rourke Press, Inc.

David Armentrout specializes in nonfiction writing and has had several book series published for primary schools. He resides in Cincinnati with his wife and two children.

PHOTO CREDITS

© Gordon Wiltsie: cover, page 19; © Bob Firth/International Stock: page 4; © East Coast Studios: pages 6, 9, 10, 13, 16, 21, 22; © Tony Gray: page 7; © Dusty Willison/International Stock: page 12; © Chuck Mason/International Stock: page 15; © Hal Kern/International Stock: page 18

EDITORIAL SERVICES:
Penworthy Learning Systems

Library of Congress Cataloging-in-Publication Data

Armentrout, David, 1962-
   Fishing / David Armentrout.
      p. cm. — (Outdoor adventures)
   Includes bibliographical references (p.24) and index.
   Summary: Briefly describes the equipment, techniques, safety, laws and tournaments involved in both freshwater and saltwater fishing.
   ISBN 1-57103-204-5
   1. Fishing—Juvenile literature. [1. Fishing.] I. Title II. Series:
Armentrout, David. 1962- Outdoor adventures.
SH445.A75 1998
799.1—dc21   98–4289
                                                                                 CIP
                                                                                 AC

Printed in the USA

TABLE OF CONTENTS

SPORTFISHING

Fishing is a popular sport. Sportfishing, also called **angling** (ANG gling), is a form of entertainment. People enjoy sportfishing because it is relaxing and a great way to enjoy the outdoors. People who fish are called anglers.

Two basic types of fishing are freshwater fishing and saltwater fishing. Freshwater fishing is done in ponds, lakes, streams, and rivers. Saltwater fishing is done in the ocean. Different types of fish are found in fresh and salt water.

It is good to have an experienced angler teach you how to fish.

RODS AND REELS

The basic fishing gear, called **tackle** (TAK ul), includes a pole, or rod, and a reel. Most fishing rods are made with man-made materials that are lightweight and easy to use. Some rods are made in one piece; others are made in sections that can be taken apart.

A rod for catching small freshwater fish is smaller than a rod for fishing in the ocean.

A heavy-duty rod and reel is used to fish in the ocean.

Fishing rods come in many styles and sizes for different types of fishing. For example, strong, heavy rods are used to catch strong, fighting ocean fish like sailfish and marlin.

A reel is used to wind in the fishing line. The reel is fastened to the fishing rod close to the handle. Reels come in many styles too.

HOOK, LINE, AND SINKER

A tackle box holds fishing supplies. The most common things found in a tackle box are hooks, lines, and sinkers.

A hook is used to hold **bait** (BAYT). Most hooks are made of steel. Hooks also come in different sizes and kinds.

Fishing line is a strong thread usually made of **nylon** (NY lahn). The strength of fishing line is measured by the number of strings it is made of. Lightweight, or fine, fishing line is used with lightweight fishing rods.

A **sinker** (SING ker) is a weight that is fastened to the fishing line. Sinkers help the hook and line drop, or sink, into the water. Sinkers are made of lead and come in many sizes.

Learn to choose the right sinker for the bait you use.

BAIT

Bait is put on a hook at the end of the fishing line. Bait is used to attract fish. Anglers use natural, or live, bait or man-made bait, called **lures** (LOORZ).

Worms, insects, and frogs are common live baits used for freshwater fishing. Anglers often use pieces of fish, shrimp, and crab when fishing in salt water. The bait you choose will depend on the type of fishing you do.

Lures look like natural fish food. Lures may be made of wood, plastic, rubber, or metal.

Fishing flies, another type of bait, look like the insect. Bird feathers are sometimes used to make flies. Lures and flies are made in a mix of colors, shapes, and sizes.

Lures come in many sizes and shapes.

FISHING METHODS

There are three basic methods of sportfishing—still fishing, trolling, and casting. To still fish, an angler sits on shore or in an anchored boat and sinks a line into the water.

Trolling is moving a boat slowly through the water as the baited hook drifts along underwater.

Docks are a good place to find fish.

When casting your line, be sure not to snag someone with your hook.

Casting means throwing a baited line into the water. The purpose is to cast your line where the fish are. Freshwater fish tend to swim in gentle pools, near rocks, or in weeds.

Casting can be done from the shore or from a boat when saltwater fishing. Anglers fishing in fresh water can cast from a boat or riverbank, or wade out to a favorite fishing hole.

LEARNING TO FISH

How do you learn to fish? Begin by having a friend or family member show you how to bait a hook and cast a line. You can practice casting in the backyard or at a nearby creek.

Beginners sometimes use a **bobber** (BAHB er) on the fishing line. A bobber floats on the water's surface while the baited hook sinks. When a fish nibbles the bait, the bobber will move. That's your sign to pull up on the line and reel in the fish.

Fishing is a sport that calls for patience and practice. To learn more about fishing, you can read fishing magazines and join fishing clubs.

An experienced angler can show you how to cast and watch your line for a bite.

FISHING SAFELY

People who fish need to follow simple safety rules.

Cuts or scrapes from hooks or other tackle are common fishing injuries. Always carry a well-stocked first-aid kit.

Sunscreen should be used even on cloudy days.

Never fish during a thunderstorm. Lightning is a killer and often strikes near water.

Fishing takes energy, just like other outdoor sports. Be sure to bring food and water for yourself.

Always wear a life jacket when fishing from a boat or when wading in a river.

Make sure you have a life jacket that fits before going out in a boat.

FISHING LAWS

Each state has its own **game laws** (GAYM LAWZ) laws. Game laws say when certain kinds of fish can be caught and how many fish can be taken. Many states require a fishing **license** (LY sens).

Always obey the local boating laws when fishing from a boat. These laws are meant to protect you and others.

Fish that are too small are often put back in the water.

Some state laws require children to wear a life vest in a boat.

Besides game laws, there are a few unwritten laws that anglers follow. Respect other anglers in the area. Do not crowd their fishing spot, and keep quiet so you do not scare the fish away.

Respect nature by not littering. Take all trash, supplies, and unused bait with you when you leave.

FISHING CONTESTS

Organized fishing is very popular. There are many fishing clubs in the U.S. The Bass Anglers Sportsman Society (B.A.S.S.), for example, has over 600,000 members.

The International Game Fish Association (IGFA) keeps records of the largest fish caught in the world. There are **tournaments** (TOOR nuh munts) for both freshwater fishing and saltwater fishing. Prizes go to anglers who catch the most fish or the heaviest fish of a certain kind.

People of all ages can enter a fishing contest.

GLOSSARY

angling (ANG gling) — to fish with a hook and line

bait (BAYT) — something, usually food, placed on a hook to attract fish

bobber (BAHB er) — a small plastic ball fastened to a line that tells anglers when a fish is ready to bite

game laws (GAYM LAWZ) — a rule to protect fish or animals by saying when, how, and how many may be captured

license (LY sens) — a permit; a card showing that you have been approved

lures (LOORZ) — man-made bait

nylon (NY lahn) — a strong elastic man-made material used to make cloth, yarn, and plastics

sinker (SING ker) — a weight used to sink a fishing line

tackle (TAK ul) — fishing gear

tournaments (TOOR nuh munts) — a series of contests

These kids fish in a saltwater canal.

INDEX

FURTHER READING

Find out more about Outdoor Adventures with these helpful books and information sites:

Steinberg, Dick (Contributing Writer). *Secrets of the Fishing Pros/The Hunting and Fishing Library.* Cy DeCosse Inc., 1989.

Schaffner, Herbert A. *Saltwater Game Fish of North America.* Gallery Books, 1989.

Field and Stream Magazine (also found at Internet address http://www.fieldandstream.com)